of

African American Inventors

Illustrator: Laura Ortega
and
Editors: Beverly A. Evans and Rosemary Carter

AuthorHouse™
1663 Liberty Drive
Bloomington, IN 47403
www.authorhouse.com
Phone: 1-800-839-8640

The illustrations and names of inventors are the author's and illustrator's interpretation/opinion and not
necessarily those of the actual inventor. The author diligently sought to find the actual name of the inventors.
By no means does this book incorporate the many inventions made by African American inventors.

Published by AuthorHouse 06/24/2013

ISBN: 978-1-4817-6238-0 (sc)
ISBN: 978-1-4817-6239-7 (e)

authorHOUSE®

Aa

A is for Airship. An airship is a self-propelled, lighter-than-air craft that flies in the sky. If you look up to the sky you will see the airship pass by.

B. F. Jackson

Bb

B is for Boot. On a snowy or rainy day children love to wear their boots out to play.

Wilson Burwell

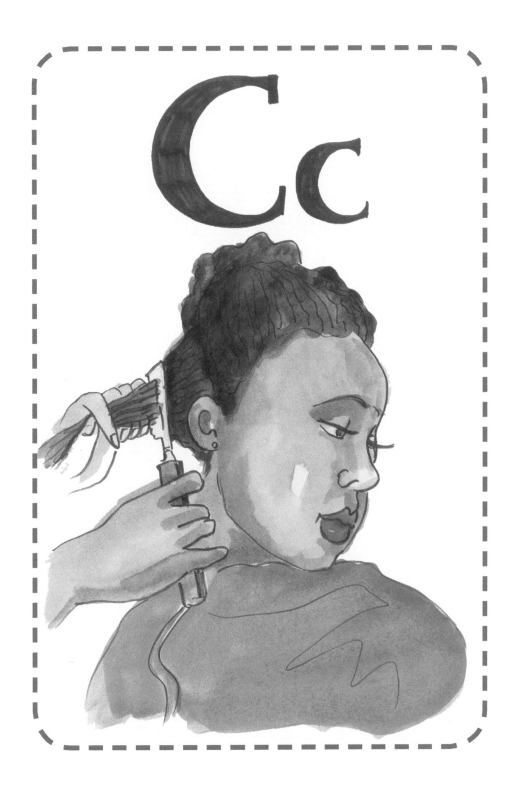

Cc

C is for Comb. A heating comb was invented to loosen the locks in our hair and to shorten the time we spend in a hairdresser's chair.

Sarah Walker

Dd

D is for Dustpan. After we sweep the floor we use the dustpan to pick up dirt by the door.

L.P. Ray

Ee

E is for Elevator. When you are in a building and want to
get to higher floors use an elevator that's hidden behind a
sliding door.

Alexander Miles

(improved elevator method)

Ff
F is for Fire Extinguisher. The fire extinguisher is used to put out a small fire or flame to prevent a big fire that can do damage just the same.
Thomas Martin

Gg

G is for Gas Mask. A gas mask is used to prevent the smell of bad gases and chemicals. Firemen use a gas mask to complete their task.

Garrett Morgan

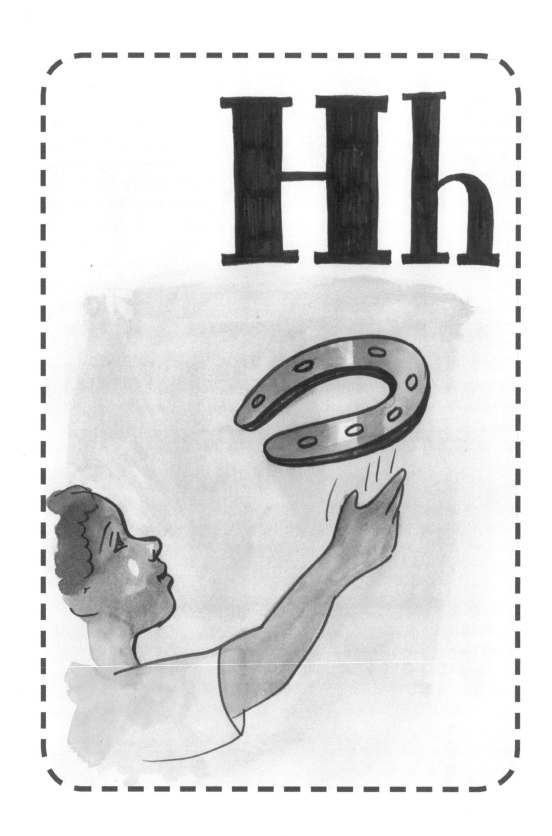

Hh

H is for Horse Shoe. To play a game of toss use a horse
shoe and be the boss.

Oscar Brown

Ii

I is for Ironing Board. Before I go out to play, dad presses
my clothes so that I can look nice all day.
Sarah Boone

Jj

J is for Jack. The jack was used to help build shoes. For smelly broken shoes, place them in jack to help build them back.

AR Cooper

Kk

K is for Key Identifier. To help sort your keys place them
inside of the identifier, if you please.
Lutrell Denson, Patent Pending

Ll

L is for Lawn Mower. When our grass grows higher we cut
it lower, thanks to the use of a lawn mower.
John Albert Burr

Mm

M is for Mailbox. When we need to send our letters across the land, we put them in the mailbox as quick as we can.

William Barry

(mail canceling machine)

Nn

N is for Nursery Chair. A nursery chair is used to rock babies. Don't despair when you want to rock your baby. Just sit in the chair and rub your baby's hair.

Oo

Oo

O is for Oil Cup. An oil cup catches the oil that mechanics
drain from a passenger or freight train.

E. J. Mc Coy

Pp

P is for Pencil Sharpener. If you have a broken pencil, do not be ashamed. Place it inside of the pencil sharpener and begin to work again.

J. L. Love

Qq

Qq

Q is for Quilt Frame. Everyone loves to stay warm during cold winter nights. Some use a quilt that is red, blue and white.

T. Elkins

Rr

R is for Railway Signal. When the train passes through our
city, the signals let us know if it is safe for us to go.
Albert B. Blackburn

Ss

S is for Shoe. When we have shoes on our feet we can hop, skip and jump to the beat.

Jan Matzeliger

(shoe lasting machine)

Tt

T is for Tricycle. Oh how I love to ride my tricycle. I ride
up and down the hills and look up high to see the sky.

M. A. Cherry

Uu

Uu

U is for Underground Railroad. When the slaves wanted to
be free, Harriet Tubman and others helped them to flee
Conductors.

Vv

V is for Video Commander. Video commanders are for our use. We love to make videos of our youth.

Joseph N. Jackson

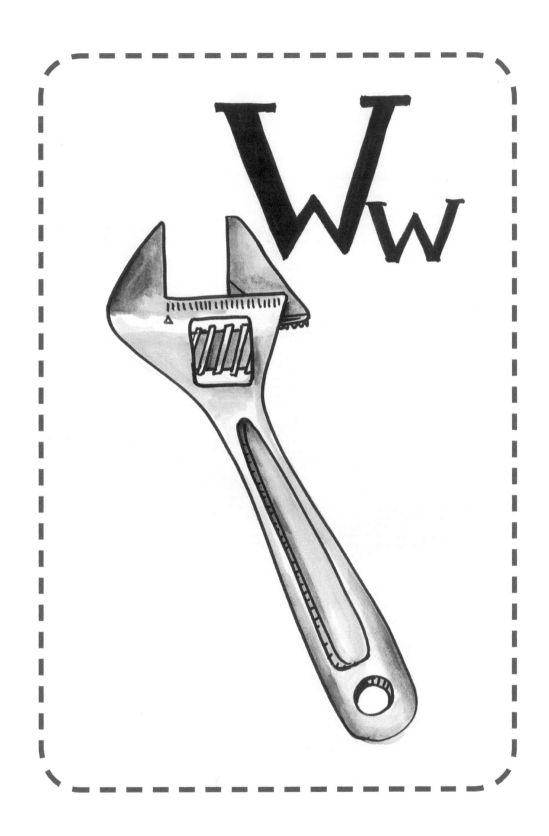

Ww

W is for Wrench. This tool is used as a fastener to turn
bolts and pipes on our cars and bikes.

J. Jackson

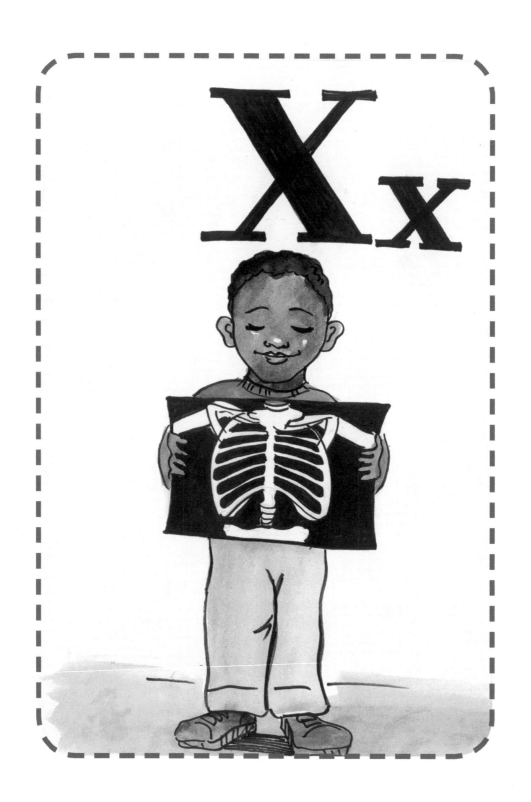

Xx

X is for X-ray Machine. Doctors use x-ray machines to look at the tiny bones that are inside of our body.

Fred Jones

(Spectrometer)

Yy

Y is for Yarn Holder. Have a spool of yarn? Place the yarn
on the holder to prevent it from rolling over.
Julian Hammond

Zz

Z is for a Z-Sleeve. In Arizona it gets so hot I wear my
z-sleeve to prevent the sun's plot.
Donna Robinson, Patent Pending

CPSIA information can be obtained
at www.ICGtesting.com
Printed in the USA
LVHW071549120819
627347LV00003B/65/P